Günther Dichatschek

Collection 8 Digitization

Günther Dichatschek

Collection 8 Digitization

Aspects of a subject area of pedagogy

ScienciaScripts

Imprint

Cover image: www.ingimage.com

This book is a translation from the original published under ISBN 978-3-639-63058-9.

Publisher:
Sciencia Scripts
is a trademark of
Dodo Books Indian Ocean Ltd. and OmniScriptum S.R.L publishing group

120 High Road, East Finchley, London, N2 9ED, United Kingdom
Str. Armeneasca 28/1, office 1, Chisinau MD-2012, Republic of Moldova, Europe
Managing Directors: Ieva Konstantinova, Victoria Ursu
info@omniscriptum.com

Printed at: see last page
ISBN: 978-620-8-38231-5

Table of contents

Acknowledgments

I would like to thank Helmut Leitner for 20 years of smooth cooperation in the "Network against Violence - Network for Education" and the many impulses in a digital world.

August 2024 Günther Dichatschek IT - Note

- http://www.netzwerkgegengewalt.org/wiki.cgi?

Introduction

The term "digitalization" evokes a wide variety of reactions. On the one hand, there are visions of a better and fairer world in the future; on the other, there are fears of change and even fear of electronic machines.

An attempt at a simple definition should help. Digitization is the conversion and presentation of information into files using electronic information technology such as computers, cell phones, Internet applications and various file databases.

More or less unnoticed, digitalized technology has become an everyday companion and part of modern society in recent decades. Further development is taken for granted; a modern society needs technological progress as a matter of course.

The starting point for the following considerations is the completion of the offline
- Course "Digital tools for adult educators"/ Graz University of Technology, CONEDU, Werde Digital.at, Federal Ministry of Education (2017) and analysis of specialist literature. The author would like to thank his digital companions for their input on this topic.

The study does not claim to be exhaustive. It is divided into four parts: general digitalization, digital learning and teaching, artificial intelligence and networking.

Part I Digitization

1 Introduction

In the 1990s, the Briton Tim BERNERS - LEE developed the text-based markup language HTML (Hyper Text Markup Language) and thus created the basis for the World Wide Web. He made his WWW software freely accessible worldwide.

At the beginning of the millennium, hardware became more mobile, easier to handle and easier to use. At that time, the joy of the possibilities of a new technology prevailed; information and messages could be exchanged, knowledge shared and business conducted regardless of time and place.

In 2004, the author joined the "Network against Violence - Network for Education". In 2007, adult educators were able to complete an offline "Digital Tools" course. A distance learning course was completed in 2018 and 2020. The opportunities and benefits were clear.

The principles of openness and participation were and are not without danger. Digital technology enables encroachment, surveillance and control.

The coronavirus pandemic has given digitalization a major boost in 2020. Home schooling, working from home, flexible working models and video conferencing have been implemented.

The expansion of opportunities and their necessity to ensure equal opportunities became clear.

The interest of educational reform efforts and political education is certainly there.

2 Communication, mass media and Public

2.1 Communication

Computers became more widespread in the 1990s, followed by internet connections. Smartphones and mobile devices arrived at the turn of the millennium.

The development shows a change in private and public communication.

The availability and presentation of information has been subject to change ever since.

The public debate is influenced as a component of democratic culture and society.

The new forms of information exchange can be seen in social networks, news services for smartphones, video platforms or web and microblogs as part of the "social web".

Communication now overlapped in terms of time and place, and publishing became possible. New media genres such as podcasts and video blogs are used by amateurs, publishers, media houses and freelance journalists.

The flood of information can hardly be recorded or sorted. Algorithmic systems take care of this and act as "digital intermediaries". They select what is displayed according to defined criteria.

Texts are available online, films and music are offered on streaming platforms. Many TV and radio stations offer their own live streams of content that they play in linear programs. Algorithmic systems also play an important role here.

2.2 Mass media

Technological change is creating new opportunities and conditions for the established mass media.

- All those involved are faced with condensed production processes and increasing time pressure.
- Robot journalism", understood as the use of learning algorithmic systems, generates short news items and reports and changes the rhythm of journalistic work.
- Journalism in traditional mass media does of course exist. The relevant media align their products to target groups. Accordingly, they offer advertising in the media formats that serve to finance them.
- Competition arises from free information on the "social web" (cf. the sometimes unsecured sources).

2.3 The public

Advancing digitalization is changing the way we deal with services and the nature of public debates.

Traditional mass media filter information in editorial offices and form opinions in the form of comments, interviews and readers' opinions. Journalism is bound by a "code of honor" (see freedom of the press, accuracy, distinctiveness, exertion of influence, protection of personality, privacy, discrimination > ●https://www.presserat.at [28.7.21]).

In the social web, algorithmic systems sort the information and decide what appears in the "feeds" (digital news).

Disinformation and hate speech (targeted defamation) are particular problem areas.

3 Society, culture and Education

Technological change is also changing our lives, cultural practices, educational needs and opportunities and creating new possibilities.

3.1 Society and Technology

Digital technology is part of our everyday lives, even if we do not use the Internet (e.g. barcodes on goods, codes when receiving parcels, digital control systems for heating, cell phone use, timekeeping, control systems in cars and rail transport).

Algorithms influence consumption/advertising, opinion-forming, everyday habits, advisory and support systems, business and economic models, changed work processes and, as a result, leisure behavior.

This influence often remains unreflected.

This is linked to the high degree of internalization of individual attitudes (socialization, education and social status).

3.2 Changing cultural practices

The influence of new technology is changing lives and everyday life.

- Users of social networks are used to presenting and staging themselves. This is part of everyday culture, especially among younger people.
- Personal statements and a sometimes emotional discourse are

published.

- Photos, short films of experiences with greetings to loved ones and friends are posted online.

- There are variations in the type of platforms. Professional networks emphasize skills and professionalism, social networks sensitivities, international networks present comparisons, supra-regional programs and opportunities for cooperation.

- News portals are used on a daily basis. The international daily press, TV stations and our own portals provide a constant supply of news and have become the norm.

- Digitization facilitates the publication of results and their exchange in education and science.

3.3 Education

The changes require media and digital skills ("digital literacy") (cf. NASSEHI 2009).

The European Commission summarizes the importance and necessity in five areas (see izbp 3/2020, 20-21)

- Information and data literacy - relevance of sources and content

- Communication and cooperation - participation in society and own identity

- Content creation online - integration of existing knowledge bases and copyright or licenses

- Security - knowledge of the protection of content, personal data and privacy

- Problem solving - identification of needs and problem areas with solution processing

There is agreement on the acquisition in school and extracurricular education.

A functioning digital infrastructure in educational institutions is a prerequisite. Devices and networks need to be managed and maintained. The practice at some schools and universities of bringing mobile devices from home ("Bring Your Own Device" / BYOD) for use in lessons and teaching requires the protection of learners' and students' personal data and clarification of the conditions of admission (cf. licenses and copyrights, for example).

Other learning opportunities are of increasing interest, such as MOOCs (Massive Open Online Courses), which offer courses for everyone (open), usually free of charge on the Internet with confirmation of participation. The basic principle is that education is a common good.

Numerous distance learning courses are subject to the respective state recognition regulations for certification. They require and need teaching and study materials, study guidance and counseling, examination regulations, and are usually subject to a fee with participation or tuition fees and a specified study framework or time frame (see the author's contribution http://www.netzwerkgegengewalt.org/wiki.cgi?Fernstudium).

4 Economy and Work

Digitalization is automating work in industrial production and networking work processes in the service sector. This is leading to a change in work processes and job profiles. New economic models and business models are emerging.

4.1 Automation and networking

These changes are often referred to as the "fourth industrial revolution" ("Industry 4.0"). People no longer control individual machines; instead, they increasingly monitor production at a central point.

Production robots and driverless transport vehicles are used as hardware. Special software is used to plan and optimize self-controlled production processes.

In Industry 4.0, all components of production are recorded and networked via the Internet. The entire work process is automated, from goods purchasing and production through to delivery (cf. the production chain in the automotive industry, for example). Industrial companies in Austria are currently working in this way in selective approaches.

In the service sector, certain areas of activity are developing as a result of the new technology. Think, for example, of bonus programs at health insurance companies, customer advice and bookings at travel agencies and railroads. US companies, for example, have gained global significance through the automation and use of new technology.

Their offerings range from advertising, IT services, sales platforms, communication offerings, streaming and distribution services.

4.2 Changes in the professional world

Digitalization is changing work, the production process and fields of employment. New qualifications are required to maintain the technology and monitor production and work processes. Control functions and safeguards are becoming increasingly important.

Shifts in the labor market between 2014 and 2030 in Germany (source: izpb 3/2020, 39)

Sectors with losses	Minus	Plus	Sectors with growth
		+425.000	Business-related services
		+335.000	Social services, homes
		+250.000	Placement of workers
		+238.000	Healthcare
		+258.000	Legal/tax advice
		+125.000	Education/ Teaching
		+73.000	IT services
Retail trade	-70.000		
Metal professions	-169.000		
Accommodation/ Hospitality	-244.000		
Mechanical engineering	-285.000		
Public administration	-372.000		

Changes and new economic and business models are coming in the area of business and work.

A shift from employment relationships to precarious working models is described. Young people, women, migrants and people without professional qualifications are particularly affected.

In terms of vocational pedagogy in the context of civic education, qualified basic vocational training and subsequently adapted further and advanced training appear to be necessary (cf. RIFKIN 2005, DICHATSCHEK 2021).

5 Estonia

The country (and the Baltic region) has long been known for its pioneering role in digitalization, particularly in the area of citizen services. For years, almost all government affairs with more than 3,000 services have been transferred to the Internet.

The key to the digital possibilities is the citizen card, which also serves as an ID card, driving license and insurance card.

The range of services continues to grow, and in future many things will be automated. For example, in the event of a birth, the hospital immediately registers the newborn with the authorities, as well as with health insurance (there is only one in Estonia), social benefits (child benefit, allowances) with feedback to the parents on their future entitlements.

This is not possible for three services in Estonia. Marriage and divorce are exempt for ethical reasons. Personal attendance is also required when buying a property and notarization at the notary.

Estonians have been able to vote online since 2005. There are danger areas for this form of digitization.

- In 2007, there were serious cyber attacks that paralyzed many Internet services.
- In 2009, several Internet services were unavailable because rats had gnawed on a terminal cable in Tallinn.

The personal impressions of a digitized civil society in the Baltic States and especially in Estonia result from an ERASMUS study semester of a daughter in the winter semester 2018/2019 in Riga (Latvia) with stays in Lithuania and Estonia.

Source: izpb 3/2020, 70

6 Bibliography Digitization

The titles that are used and/or directly quoted in the article are listed.

Federal Agency for Civic Education (ed.): Series Aus Politik und Zeitgeschichte No. 18-19/2016, Arbeit und Digitalisierung, Bonn

Federal Agency for Civic Education (ed.): Information on Civic Education/ izpb 3/2020, Digitalization, Bonn

Dichatschek G. (2019): Media work. Aspects of further education in the context of civic education/media education-media education, Saarbrücken

Dichatschek G. (2021): Vocational orientation - theory, practice and fields of action, aspects of the transition from school to the world of work, Saarbrücken

Opinion of the Data Ethics Commission, October 2019 > https://datenethikkommission.de (27.7.21)

Nassehi A. (2009): Patterns: theory of the digital society, Munich Otto

Ph. - Graf E. (ed.) (2018): 3TH1CS the ethics of the digital age, Bonn

Rifkin J. (2005): The end of work and its future, Frankfurt/M.

Rosenbach M. - Stark H. (2014): The NSA - Complex. Edward Snowden and the path to total surveillance, Munich

Schmidt J. H. (2018): Social Media, Wiesbaden

Part II Digital learning and teaching

1 Preliminary remark

The following explanations on the topics of "learning and teaching with technologies" are based on the importance of the various applications, areas of use, perspectives and technologies. The increasing use requires an examination of the subject area in an interdisciplinary approach.

The starting point for the considerations are the

- Completion of the online - course "Digital tools for adult educators"/ TU Graz, CONEDU (2017),
- Completion of the distance learning courses Adult Education and Sustainable Development/ Comenius Institute - Münster (2018, 2020) and
- Discussion of the specialist literature.

The considerations are based exclusively on personal interest, a long history of networking and are intended as an introduction to a wide range of topics.

As an introduction to an interdisciplinary subject area of technology-supported learning and teaching, the course begins with basic concepts.

German-language manuals are helpful as an introduction to online learning ISSING - KLIMSA 2008, to e-learning HOHENSTEIN - WILBERS 2002, innovative learning systems KUHLMANN - SAUTER 2008, educational science as an introduction to teaching and learning with media STRITTMATTER - NIEGEMANN 2000.

The study is based on EBNER - SCHÖN 2011 and the online course "Digital tools for adult educators" by TU Graz/ CONEDU 2017.

Learning technologies initially comprise digital devices and applications to support learning and teaching, such as presentation technology (overhead projector, slide projector), communication technology (telephone, fax), computer technology (PC, laptop), Internet technology (e-mail, World Wide Web) and sensor technologies (RFID, GPS for cell phones).

- E-learning - learning and teaching situations in connection with computers and the Internet (often networks),
- Online learning - learning and teaching situations for internet and intranet-supported distance learning,
- Blended learning - face-to-face teaching supplemented with online phases,
- Wikis - learning and teaching situations with content from several users, but not simultaneously editable,
- formal learning (guided learning), non-formal learning (self-directed learning) and informal learning (natural learning in everyday life),
- lifelong learning - lifelong learning and teaching

The main reference disciplines are educational psychology and computer science. Smaller subject areas are media education, vocational education, personnel development, education management and organizational development.

The topics include an introduction, digitalization, technical overview, distance learning, didactics, media pedagogy, media-based learning, performance assessment and learning and teaching with adults. The breadth of the subject area can be recognized by the related disciplines.

2 Digitization

The phenomena of change and education systems are discussed below.

2.1 Phenomena of change

The electrical (e-Mail, e-Car, AT), informational (i-X, iPad) and digital are increasingly permeating our world, in the sense of "uniquituous computing" (ubiquitous computer) right down to the communication-capable chip in the ski lift ticket and in every product. The loudspeaker is becoming a voice recognition terminal (Alexa), the refrigerator of the future "knows" what it contains, the person-free supermarket checkout of the future "reads" the contents of the shopping cart by communicating with the products.

Orwell's "1984" is surpassed several times over. Every cell phone locates its wearer and tends to eavesdrop on its surroundings with a microphone and camera. The smartwatch/fitness watch listens to every heartbeat and step and logs and signals stress and sleep quality.

Inventions or events have a long-term influence on development, often over the course of centuries, even in the form of a life cycle. Just think of agriculture, the Iron Age, sailing ships and electricity. The development and use of the computer is also in the midst of a stormy development, the end of which is often assumed to be near, but is currently not foreseeable in terms of content or time in 2022.

Digitization as the utilization of computer technologies is a marathon, a "moving target", not something that can be done. This development is illustrated by an example. Starting in 2020Q4, Apple is setting new standards with "Apple Silicon" and pushing the boundaries of what is feasible on inexpensive end-user PCs/tablets/smartphones. The transition to the 5 nm manufacturing process enables even more highly integrated, more powerful, more energy-efficient and more cost-effective CPUs. The CPU is upgraded to a SOC (system on chip), additional components are added to the CPU: powerful GPUs (graphic processor unit) and, for the first time, special processors that support ML (machine learning, neural networks such as speech recognition and image recognition) with high performance. In this way, 32 processors are now working in parallel in the first M1 chip. This represents an almost disruptive leap in development, with a claim to market leadership that will shake up the competition (Indel, AMD, Nividia) and force massive reactions/innovations/price reductions.

For digital learning and teaching, this means a further push towards more powerful and cheaper mobile devices in 2021-2022, combined with software products such as learning software with easy usability and high-quality artificial intelligence.

2.2 Education systems and Digitalization

Education systems are sluggish systems that lag behind developments. This applies to Austria in comparison to the cosmopolitan, competitive (competition-oriented) Germany and the financially strong, economically savvy, participative and democratic Switzerland.

Accordingly, the following would be necessary

- a reform and flexibilization of the education system as a goal in itself (lifelong learning, further qualification of teachers),

- a reform of content with transparent reassessment of all knowledge modules and skills,
- Prerequisite for new subjects and subject networks,
- Sufficient and evenly flowing budget funds for digitization of education as a permanent task,
- Not to marginalize other reform needs such as teacher training, migration and school architecture,
- leverage digital potential with more participation and collaboration and
- education to promote individual strengths and vibrant diversity with the involvement of all stakeholders.

3 Technical Overview

It addresses end devices in the educational process and teaching in their use, historically from the chalkboard to the PC - laptop - netbook (cf. precisely EBNER - SCHÖN 2017, 23-30).

- Chalkboard - goes back to James Pillans (1778 - 1864) (cf. WAGNER 2014, 170)
- Whiteboards - further development from 1990 used with special felt-tip pens
- Slide projectors - developed by Leitz (Wetzlar) in 1926, slides and slide strips are projected onto a surface through a lens
- Daylight projector (overhead projector) - developed in 1960 for transparent transparencies for a projection surface in daylight, eye contact between teacher and audience
- Epiprojectors (episcope) - projection of opaque paper ("incident light projection")
- Televisions, video recorders, DVD players - Televisions go back to a patent by Paul Nipkow in 1886, followed by flat screens of various sizes - Video recorders record and play back films, followed by the high-capacity DVD player in 1996

- Touchscreen - interaction with a computer by touching the screen, formerly often used in info monitors and ATMs, today in cell phones, tablet PCs, laptops and MP3 players
- Video projector ("Beamer") - video signal from a computer or DVD player on a screen
- PC, laptop, netbook - first electronic computer developed by Konrad Zuse around 1938 - 1945, modern computers are based on John von Neumann in the forties, the first laptop as a mobile PC was presented by IBM in 1975, the netbook as the smallest version often has only a low performance
- Interactive pen displays - touch-sensitive screen with pen, comparable to a tablet computer
- Cell phones - with the smartphone as a cell phone and extended functionality of personal digital assistants, the devices are equipped with a high-resolution camera, Internet, GPS modules and touch displays, first smartphone developed by IBM in 1992 ("Simon")
- Current and future technologies - the most important future technology is the tablet computer in its current form as the Apple iPad.

Multi-touch technology was first used in 2005 for a mixing console control panel. This was followed by today's familiar "slates" (tablet computers without an external keyboard).

The diversity of technologies in teaching and educational processes points to further possibilities. In general, there are always difficulties and skepticism in the use, the further path in technological progress is clear, taking into account media pedagogy and engineering pedagogy in connection with computer science (cf. WAGNER 2014, MELEZINEK 1977).

4 Distance learning

The function of interaction, spatial and temporal flexibility with possible didactics is differentiated as a development in three generations (development stages), from around 1850 the correspondence generation, from around 1960 the telecommunications or open university generation and the computer and Internet generation from around 1990.

Subsequently, developments in online learning and more recent developments in mobile and collaborative learning must be taken into account (cf. PETERS 1997, 27; EBNER - SCHÖN 2027, 45-53).

4.1 Media-supported learning

Technology-supported learning is media-supported learning. Learning is closely related to teaching; the basic learning theory is formed by a learning culture and didactics.

Media enable a broader knowledge of content and learning techniques. Communication and feedback as a social process between learners and teachers as well as contact between learners result in modern interaction through ICT (information and communication technology).

The development of the Internet and the didactic possibilities for online learning resulted in a paradigm shift.

- Meanwhile, universities offer online courses and degree programs.
- There is e-learning in schools, in adult education in the quaternary education sector and in company training (see DICHATSCHEK 2017, 2018; online course "Digital tools for adult educators"/ TU Graz, CONEDU 2017).

Distance learning is characterized by the spatial and temporal separation of teachers and learners, media enable learning processes, interaction and flexibility. The didactic options and content on offer are different, as are the certification options and participant fees.

4.2 Technological Innovations

According to GARRISON (1985, 239-240; quoted from EBNER - SCHÖN 2017, 46)
three generations/development phases of technological innovation are distinguished as a paradigm shift in learning and teaching in distance learning. The main ones are print media, telecommunications media and the computer (two-channel communication), supplemented by single-channel radio, television or DVD.

- Print-based distance learning - study letters or documents for self-study (cf. LANGENSCHEIDT - TOUSSAINT French language courses with phonetic transcription and subsequently with a record), essentially without supervision in the early days and therefore not really distance learning. Great Britain founded the "University of South Africa (UNISA)" in Pretoria (SA) in 1875 as the world's first distance learning university.

- Distance learning and telecommunications

- The pioneer is the British Open University (OUUK), founded in 1969. In 1974, the distance learning university in Hagen was founded in German-speaking countries, which is still the largest university in Germany today. In the following distance learning universities, a systemic approach was applied, processes of course design, media didactic preparation and technical and organizational support for students in a process based on the division of labour. Study centers based on the OUUK model with access to technology, video conferencing, study materials, library services, student advisory services and examination centers form an important part of the support system with their establishment (Fern -Universität Hagen with 13 regional centers).

- Telecommunications media enable the transmission and communication of sound, images and text. The abundance of possibilities such as telephone, fax, TV, video and radio as well as audio, video and computer conferencing gives rise to the term "multimedia distance teaching", which is used not only in distance learning universities but also in "bush schools" in Australia, for example.

- Computer - Internet ("Computer Assisted Learning"/ CAL)

- Interaction is understood as the connection to the computer program, but without social interaction and a dialogue between learners and teachers as well as learners among themselves, programmed lessons are not very successful.

- In 1989, the Briton Tim BERNERS-LEE (CERN/ "European Organization for Nuclear Research") published a proposal with the idea of a network-based system, subsequently referred to as the "World Wide Web" (WWW). Murray TUROFF of the New Jersey Institute of Technology (1995) is regarded as the inventor of the computer conference method ("Computer M3ediated Communication"/CMC and developer of the CMC platform "Virtual Classroom". As a result, today's learning and campus management systems have evolved. Personal dialog and tools for collaborative learning and working are the most valuable contribution of the new technology to distance learning (cf. KIRKWOOD 1998, 1228-241, cited in EBNER - SCHÖN 2017, 50).

4.3 Technology-supported learning

Online learning or e-learning developed strongly in the mid-1990s. The USA is a good example, with 2.9 million students enrolled in online courses in 2007 (cf. ALLEN - SEAMAN 2008 > http://www.sloan-c.org/publications/survey/pdf/staying_the_course.pdf [7.1.21]).

As a result, more and more younger people decided to study online after leaving school, with the 25 to 44 age group being the largest. In the USA, face-to-face universities have become increasingly expensive and the need to earn money has made part-time study an affordable educational option.

Mobile devices such as cell phones and tablet computers enable e-learning on the PC and just-in-time access to knowledge and information. The democratic education process is thus experiencing an increase in its level of development.

4.4 Collaborative learning on the web 2.0

Web 2.0 is a term used to describe new interactive applications on the Internet and WWW. Users can create content themselves. Examples include wikis, blogs and social tagging (collaborative indexing) as well as image and video sharing portals.

Cooperative learning offers itself (cf. ERPENBECK - SAUTER 2007). A large number of web offerings are emerging that do not have their own database, but rather combine data from third parties in new services ("mash-up"). User creativity is becoming an essential element. Examples include Wikipedia and Flicker. The boundaries between producers and consumers from the Web 1.0 phase are disappearing. "Social networks" such as Xing, Facebook, StudiVZ and YouTube as well as communication media such as blogs create spaces for communication on the Internet (cf. WOLLING 2009, 7 -18).

"Personal Learning Environments (PLE) are web-based mashups with an individual learning environment. The self-directed and active learning of students is becoming more central (cf. SCHAFFERT - KALZ 2008, 1-24).

5 Didactics

Learning theories form an important basis for didactic decisions and teaching strategies. Paradigms include behaviorism, cognitivism, constructivism and, to a limited extent, connectivism (cf. EBNER - SCHÖN 2017, 93).

The objectives of a teaching project are decisive for the implementation or design strategy; an analysis of the objectives is supported by teaching objective taxonomies. Two classic formats are presentational and exploratory teaching in conjunction with an appropriate learning environment.

5.1 Introduction

Today, didactics is defined in educational science as the science of teaching and learning (cf. KLAFKI 1995, 92-93). The distinction between didactics and methodology as a concept hardly plays a role today. In vocational education and training, didactics is often equated with a systematic approach to teaching. The interaction between teachers, learners and teaching content is assumed (cf. "didactic triangle").

Teaching is understood as goal-oriented behavior or action (cf. STRITTMATTER - NIEGEMANN 2000, 9-10). Teaching functions include motivation and motivation, conveying information, ensuring understanding and processing, ensuring the retention and recollection of content, the extent and composition as well as the sequencing (sequence), ensuring the transfer of knowledge (application of knowledge) to new tasks and situations and guidance for realization (supervision and support).

In modern teaching and learning research, the term "scaffolding" is used in such teaching measures to help learners gain their own insights (cf. SHUELL 1996, 752). The following learning functions initiated by learners and/or the learning environment are intended to achieve the desired learning success, such as generating expectations, motivating, activating prior knowledge, directing attention, encoding (memorizing cognitive content), comparing, generating hypotheses, repeating, receiving feedback, receiving evaluations, monitoring, combining and integrating what has been learned. The (subject) didactics and which sequences are to perform the learning functions remain open.

5.2 Overview Learning theories

5.2.1 Behaviorism

Behaviorism as a learning theory dominated the principles of learning psychology until the middle of the 20th century. It is based on the stimulus-response model. The brain is seen as an organ that reacts to stimuli with innate or learned behavior. New stimuli shape behavior.

In classical conditioning, a neutral stimulus is temporally coupled with a stimulus that triggers a reflex reaction; this works for physiological and emotional reactions (fear, stress; cf. WATSON - RAYNER 1920,1-14).

In operant conditioning, a spontaneous behavior is reinforced with a pleasant stimulus or the removal of unpleasant stimuli and thus shaped (cf. SKINNER 1954, 221-233). Behavior is learned by doing and imitating. BANDURA (1977) added cognitive aspects to "learning from a model".

Learning as a special form of behavior is understood as a form of training. This inevitably leads to an authoritarian role for the teacher (cf. EBNER - SCHÖN 2011, 95).

5.2.2 Cognitivism

At the beginning of the 1980s, the increasing importance of technical areas, referred to as the "information processing paradigm", led to a claim to leadership in learning theory (cf. BAUMGARTNER - PAYR 1999). Learning is regarded as a mental process that can be modeled in information processing in the computer.

Information is absorbed and processed with the acquisition of knowledge. Learning and teaching processes are mostly linguistically coded information from the sender (teacher) to the receiver (learner). The connectionist approach supplements or modifies cognitivism with biological models (cf. REY 2000).

Characteristic is the labeling and search for cognitive processes. Teachers prepare content didactically in order to facilitate information processing. The communication relationship is bidirectional (cf. BAUMGARTNER - PAYR 2004).

5.2.3 Constructivism

Variants of this learning theory refer to epistemology, neurobiology, brain research; communication science, sociology of knowledge and cognitive research (cf. PÖRKSEN 2001). Common to the scientific-theoretical approaches is the view that reality cannot be objectively perceived and described and therefore cannot be recognized without presuppositions (cf. EBNER - SCHÖN 2011, 96).

Thinking, perception and cognition are based on the constructions of an observer. Humans form a system that is connected to the environment. Our brain only reacts to information from outside that has already been processed and interpreted (autopoiesis). Learning is therefore an autopoietic process, stimulated or disturbed from the outside.

It requires learning environments with complex problems and authentic content, the stimulation of personal experience and opportunities for social exchange (cf. REUSSER 2006, 151-168). Knowledge is therefore an individual and social construct.

Field studies with participant observation and interpretative methods are intended to better understand complex phenomena. From the perspective of constructivism, people shape their environment and change it. Teaching and learning are regarded as different systems, possibly loosely connected. Accordingly, teaching appears to make little sense (cf. EBNER - SCHÖN 2011, 96). As a coach, the teacher has a head start in terms of experience and supports learning activities.

5.2.4 Connectivism

Controversial as a learning theory in its own right, connectivism understands learning as a self-organized process that takes place in networks and consists of the provision of connections.

The approach shifts to distributed knowledge for use in real and virtual networks (see MOSER 2008). The approach is based on the observation that people are more likely to create new connections in a medial and technologized world than to construct something new. Based on a rapidly changing world, having to make decisions is already seen as an act of learning.

A didactic approach to teaching is not possible here. Learners are responsible for supporting each other and using the available sources of information. At best, teachers can facilitate networks.

5.3 Teaching objective taxonomies

Objects, processes or phenomena are organized as a classification scheme with uniform rules.

A teaching objective taxonomy classifies concrete or abstract as well as subject-specific or interdisciplinary teaching objectives. Different dimensions of learning such as cognitive, emotional and motor teaching objectives can be identified. The classic example of a teaching objective taxinomy is the taxinomy developed in the 1950s by BLOOM and colleagues with cognitive, affective and psychomotor teaching objectives (cf. BLOOM - KRATHWOHL 1956).

Subsequently, ANDERSON and KRATHWOHL (2001) revised Bloom's taxonomy. Their matrix refers exclusively to cognition (factual knowledge, conceptual knowledge, process knowledge, metacognitive knowledge/knowledge about one's own knowledge).

Types of learning objectives are sometimes recommended as an alternative (cf. OSER - PATRY 1990). The learning objectives are classified neither hierarchically nor according to dimensions. Each type of learning objective is assigned to a specific form of learning and thus forms a basic model.

- Learning through personal experience and learning by discovery,
- Formation of terms and concepts to build up facts, facts and networked knowledge and
- Routine formation and skills training as the the goal of automation.

6 Media education

Media education is currently an integral part of our education system. Pedagogy and didactics are focal points. As a broad subject area, there are different trends in media education.

According to EBNER - SCHÖN (2011, 103 - 105), educational, critical-emancipative, educational-technological and action-oriented media pedagogy currently play a role. The aim is to train media skills, and Web 2.0 is becoming increasingly important.

Different subject areas and their questions influence media education, educational science, media science, journalism and communication science, psychology and sociology (cf. SWOBODA 1994, 11-24; BAACKE 2007, 4).

Educational processes include leisure time, basic and advanced training, political education, interculturality, business education and vocational education.

6.1 Trends in media education

Different currents of media education have differed over the course of time, sometimes coexisting in parallel to this day, such as the traditional preservationist, critical-emancipative, educational-technological and action-oriented positions.

- The educational preservationist position stands for protection against harmful media influences in the educational process of new media and mass media (cf. POSTMAN 2003, SPITZER 2006).

- The critical-emancipative position is based on critical theory and involves an examination of print and e-media and their power structures. The social sciences focus on politically oriented social change (cf. GANGUIN - SANDER 2008, 62). The approach lacks the practice and action orientation in which it could have been effective. The formation of a counter-public and the active political individual would be of interest for political education.

- The educational technology position is concerned with the possibilities of using media in educational processes in order to improve teaching and learning (cf. HÜTHER - PODEHL 2004, 117).

- The action-oriented position improves usage. The action-oriented media of the 1980s with citizen journalism and open channels improve the use of media, resulting in the concept of media literacy. This recognizes the context of media education with developments in society as a whole and the current participatory structure with Web 2.0 media.

6.2 Media competence

BAACKE (2007) gave the term meaning, whereby media competence was developed from the concept of "communicative competence" by Jürgen HABERMAS.

Here, the comprehensive ability of people to communicate by means of symbols of a linguistic and non-linguistic nature is understood (cf.

SCHORB 2009, 50-56). The aim is to shape and change the way people live together.

- Communication is therefore oriented towards a social reality. In the diversity of the terminology, media literacy depends on the current media technology (cf. STRITTMATTER - NIEGEMANN 2000, 38; EBNER - SCHÖN 2011, 107).
- Media studies is covered in the cognitive dimension, media use in the action orientation, media ethics in the moral dimension and media design in the aesthetic dimension.
- The development of media skills in formal learning and teaching concerns schools, universities and the extracurricular education sector of youth work and especially vocational training.

Digital media competence means active (creation, design, publication) and passive competence (consumption, evaluation, assessment) with the following special features

- Digital media tend to be mass media (worldwide access),
- almost free of charge for the individual,
- This involves considerable costs for the operators, mostly financed by income from products or user fees,
- Training providers need an IT budget and
- targeted advertising spaces and an evaluation of users ("transparent person").

7 Media-based learning

7.1 Planning and design

The conception of media-didactic teaching media in a media-based learning environment requires systematic planning and design.

In contrast to lesson planning, teaching media must be designed and developed down to the last detail as the basis for largely independent learning (cf. STRITTMATTER - NIEGEMANN 2000, 7-17). From today's perspective, the lack of reference to a psychological model of the teaching-learning process is problematic.

Another development, which is hardly used in Europe, developed in

North America. "Didactical" in North American English has a rather negative connotation. It stands for rigid and teacher-determined teaching in the style of religious Sunday school instruction (i.e. frontal - dominating - reproducing - learning by heart in the format of didactic materialism).

Planning models for educational programs distinguish between different teaching objectives and categories of teaching objectives in a specific sequence of learning steps.

This "Instructional Development Model"/ ID covers everything from school lessons to computer-supported learning environments (cf. GUSTAFSON - BRANCH 1997).

The core of this approach and theory are

- Recommendations on what to do,
- under certain general conditions with certain learning prerequisites,
- to achieve the learning objectives of a category.

7.2 Instruction

Instruction is based on instructional theories and includes demonstrating, narrating and explaining as well as materials, task requirements and reactions to learners' activities.

Instruction is thus more comprehensive than teaching and includes the development of teaching media and their use (cf. STRITTMATTER - NIEGEMANN 2000, 8). Since the 1960s, ID has developed a technology for planning and designing educational processes in the USA, including in continuing education, pioneered by Robert M. GAGNE (1985). A distinction is made between five categories of teaching objectives.

The basic principle of ID is to ensure the learning requirements for the following teaching content.

A categorization of skills is required.

- Linguistic knowledge - terms, arguments, factual knowledge and theory,
- Cognitive skills - discrimination, descriptive and abstract concepts,

rules and problem solving,

- Cognitive strategies - developing methods to improve the efficiency of thinking and learning processes,
- Attitudes - mental states when deciding on actions towards people, things and events,
- Motor skills - perform practical tasks using equipment and materials, procedures correctly and fluently in appropriate time and accuracy.

Appropriate teaching methods are recommended for the desired learning outcomes. GAGNE (1985, 245) distinguishes a specific sequence of teaching events ("teaching steps"). This refers to the necessary learning conditions for the acquisition of skills.

- Gaining attention
- Information on teaching objectives
- Activation of prior knowledge
- Presentation of the subject matter
- Learning guide
- Implementation of what has been learned
- Give feedback
- Performance monitoring and assessment
- Securing the transfer

7.3 Digital Potentials

Creating digital potential

- increased digital communication options and participation of all those involved in the education system,
- digital textbooks and teaching materials, such as a free library until the school-leaving examination, a memory stick for every citizen,
- Digital explanatory videos can be integrated into lessons,
- Development of online courses in the individual educational areas for qualifications and

• Gamification of learning content, flipped classroom (learning at home).

7.4 Technical Infrastructure

Bandwidth is the term for the amount of data in bits or bytes that can be transported over a certain data line per unit of time/second. Modern Internet connections for videos and fast downloads are referred to as "broadband" and are in the 1-1000 Mbit/s range.

Servers owned and controlled by an educational institution to provide digital support to teachers and students for digital learning and teaching in the educational institution and from home ("distance learning").

Generally available digital media collections (digital media library) form storage areas by subject area and by time period.

7.5 Development of teaching and learning situations

The M 0 0 C (Massive Open Opline Course) phenomenon refers to online courses that can be completed by a large number of learners. Such online courses became known at elite US universities and for a few years became a vision of the future of university education.

Digital education opens up development visions for rural and peripheral areas.

• Students can complete high-quality studies and degrees without having to emigrate. Broadband coverage is necessary for the establishment and relocation of companies.

• Broadband coverage is also essential to make the region attractive to newcomers to the city and tourists.

7.6 Problem areas

As a mediating position, advantages and disadvantages also apply to digital learning and teaching.

• As "learning with keyboard and screen", the social side is suppressed because learning through contact and communication is hindered by the torture of video transmission. There will probably be losers and winners, people with and without talent.

• Familiarity with digital products and tools is created, which is required both in everyday life and in business.

- The temptation to "copy and paste" makes it more difficult to read one's own work. There is a danger of such an attitude being carried through school and into university without any awareness of wrongdoing (keyword "plagiarism").

Digital learning and teaching is indispensable in certain situations that make it necessary to acquire the skills of self-organization and self-discipline. These sub-steps on the path to educational autonomy with personal responsibility and self-organization (lifelong learning) must be taken into account.

8 Performance assessment with E - Assessment - systems

After the knowledge transfer phase, computer-based examinations are becoming increasingly important.

E-assessment systems result in electronic preparation, implementation and follow-up of learning progress checks. The following section deals with didactic, methodological and organizational aspects.

- A learning progress assessment is the query, measurement and evaluation of a learner's internalized knowledge and mastery of methods. The aim is to provide information about the learning status.

- E - Assessments have to meet the requirements in the dimensions of didactics, methodology and organization (cf. GRUTTMANN 2010). Technical support must also be taken into account.

Didactics - influence on teaching and learning objectives, influences the type of learning progress control (LFK) - formative assessment with several smaller tests as part of the learning process, continuous overview of learning progress - summative assessment with achievement of the learning objective, completion of the learning phase with certification - diagnostic assessment with different forms such as learning-accompanying or selective character

Methodology - convergent tasks with precise definition of the solution (e.g. multiple choice tasks) - divergent tasks record background knowledge, solution methods and justification (e.g. free text tasks)

Organization - structuring necessary in phases

- Preparation - List of questions, List of participants, room and time allocation and data recording

- Implementation - System operation, presence and identity of the participants, information on implementation and

- Follow-up - correction of work, feedback and grade lists, archiving

E-assessment systems can bring about an improvement in efficiency and effectiveness. The three dimensions must be taken into account. The increasing need for certification with regard to performance orientation in society and in the education systems means that there is an increasing need for LFK and examinations.

9 Learning and teaching in adult education

Learning and teaching in the tertiary and quaternary education with technologies

- more self-control,

- Application orientation and flexibility,

- in the design of teaching and learning opportunities in study content, professional development and private contexts as well as lifelong learning.

To note are the existing reservations and/or or lack of institutional framework conditions. With the possibilities of Web 2.0 and increasing internationality of adult education technology-based educational processes are becoming increasingly important (see E - Platform for Adult Education in Europe/ EPALE > https://ec.europa.eu/epale/de/resource-centre/content/netzwerk-gegen-gewalt ; > https://epale.ec.europa.eu/de/node/152088 [12.01.21]).

In compared to the Anglo-Saxon countries needs there is more interesting offers.

Adult education concerns the tertiary education sector (universities) and the quaternary education sector with general adult education and the breadth of vocational adult education with vocational qualifications.

- From this perspective, educational processes are about new knowledge on the basis of previous education (cf. the importance of professional educational guidance).

- Technology meets the desire for self-direction by leading to flexibility in learning and teaching processes. Access to learning is made easier and individual learning paths are supported.

- Technology-supported learning in no way replaces the necessary interaction between learners and teachers face-to-face and does not achieve a comparable quality to face-to-face events. Blended learning concepts are the ideal solution.

- Older adults and media-savvy younger adults need to be able to use media safely and understand the added value.

- A sensible use of technology requires teachers to have media skills (cf. the importance of the online course "Digital tools for adult educators"/ TU Graz -CONEDU).

- Adult education for teachers is considered to be the least professionalized area of education, especially as the breadth of training for teachers by no means presupposes professional initial and further training (cf. for the higher education sector the internal personnel development offers or internal courses for higher education didactics; for the area of general adult education the Austrian Academy for Continuing Education, internal initial and further training offers of the individual institutions; EBNER - SCHÖN 2011, 387 - 388).

- Successful educational concepts use media and technology on several institutional and didactic levels. Web 2.0, online social networks, wikis and blogs are all possible options. Web 2.0 offers peer learning, for example, and can be integrated well into blended leaning concepts alongside other options.

The question of the future of technology-supported adult education will probably concern the following objectives in the longer term (cf. ISSING 2002).

- Political goals - Access to education

- Economic goals - increasing cost flexibility, reducing idle times

- Didactic goals - Increasing the learning efficiency and application orientation

- Content objectives - Promotion of media, self-learning and social skills

10 Bibliography Digital learning and Teaching

The titles that are used and/or directly quoted in the article are listed.

Allen E. - Seaman J. (2008): Staying the course - Online Education in the Unites States 2008

Anderson I.W. - Krathwohl D..R . (2001): A Taxanomy for learning, teaching, and assessment. A revision of Bloom's taxanomy of educational outcomes, New York

Baacke D. (2007): Medienpädagogik, Tübingen Bandura A. (1977):

Social learning theory, Prenice Hall

Baumgartner P. - Payr S. (1999): Learning with software, Innsbruck

Bloom B.S. - Krathwohl D.R. (1956): Taxanomy of educational objectivies. The classification of educational goals, Handbook I: Cognitive Domain, New York

Dichatschek G. (2017): Adult continuing education. A contribution to the theory and practice of continuing education, Saarbrücken

Dichatschek G. (2018): Learning cultures in adult and continuing education. A contribution to theory, practice and action-specific challenges in the context of civic education, Saarbrücken

Dichatschek G. (2019): Media work. Aspects of further education in the context of political education/media education - media education, Saarbrücken

Dichatschek G. (2020): Teacher education. Theory and practice of professionalizing the training of teachers, school leaders and school quality management, Saarbrücken

Die Deutsche Schule DDS, Issue 2/2017: Focus issue "Education in the digital world"

Ebner M. - Schön S. (eds.) (2011): Textbook for learning and teaching with technologies, Norderstedt

Erpenbeck J. - Sauter W. (2007): Competence Development on the Net - New Blended Learning in Web 2.0, Cologne

Ganguin S.-Sander U.(2008): Critical-emancipative media education, in: Sander U.-Gross E.-Hagger K.U. (eds.): Handbuch Medienpädagogik, Wiesbaden, 61-65

Fromme J.- Sesink W. (eds.) (2008): Pedagogical Media Theory, Wiesbaden

Gagne R.M. (1985): The conditions of learning and theory of instruction, New York

Gruttmann S. (2010): Formatives E -Assessment in der Hochschullehre - Computerunterstützte Lernfortschrittskontrollen im Informatikstudium, Münster

Gustafson G.L.-Branch R. M. (1997): Survey of instructional development models, New York

Hierczeg M. (2006): Einführung in die Medieninformatik, Munich

Hohenstein A.- Wilbers K. (2002): Handbook E - Learning, Cologne

Hüther J.-Podehl B. (2004): Geschichte der Medienpädagogik, in: Hüther J.- Schorb B.(Eds.): Grundbegriffe Medienpädagogik, Munich, 116-126

Issing I.J. (ed.) (2002): Information and Learning with Multimedia and the Internet. Textbook for study and practice, Weinheim

Issing I.J.- Klimsa P. (2008): Online Learning, Munich

Klafki W. (1995): Zum Problem der Inhalte des Lehrens und Lernens in der Schule aus der Sicht kritisch - konstruktiver Didaktik, in: Hopmann S. - Riquarts K. (eds.): Didaktik and/ or Curriculum. Basic problems of an international comparative didactics, Weinheim-Basel, 91-104

Kuhlmann A. - Sauter W. (2006): Innovative Learning Systems: Competence Development with Blended Learning and Social Software, Berlin - Heidelberg

Melezinek A. (1977): Engineering pedagogy - the practice of imparting technical knowledge, Vienna

Moser H. (2008): Introduction to network didactics. Teaching and learning in the knowledge society, Hohengehren

Oser F. - Patry J.L. (1990): Choreographies of instructional learning. Basic models of teaching. Reports on Educational Science 89, Freiburg/

Switzerland

Austrian Journal of Political Science 2006/4 : Focus issue "Media and Politics"

Peters O. (1997): Didaktik des Fernstudiums - Erfahrungen und Diskussionstand in nationaler und internationaler Sicht, Grundlagen der Weiterbildung, Berlin

Postman N. (2003): The Disappearance of Childhood, Frankfurt/ M.

Pörksen B. (2001): The Certainty of Uncertainty. Conversations on Constructivism, Heidelberg

Reusser K. (2006): Konstruktivismus - vom epistemologischen Leitbegriff zur Erneuerung didaktischer Kultur, in: Bauer M. - Fuchs M. - Füglister P. - Reusser K. - Wyss H. (eds.): Didaktik auf psychologischer Grundlage - Von Hans Aeblis kognitionspsychologischer Didaktik zur modernen Lehr - Lernforschung, Bern, 151-168

Rey G.D. (2009): E - Learning, theories, design recommendations and research, Bern

Schaffert S. - Kalz M. (2008): Personal learning environments: Fundamentals, opportunities and challenges of a new concept, in: Wilbers K. - Hohenstein A. (Eds.): Handbuch E - Learning, Deutscher Wirtschaftsdienst Köln, 1-24

Schorb B. (2009): Educated and competent. Media education instead of media competence? in: medien + erziehung 53 (5), 50-56

Sheull Th.J. (1996): Teaching and learning in a classroom context, in: Berliner D.C. - Calfee R.C. (eds.): Handbook of educational psychology, New York, 726-764

Skinner B.F.(1954): The science of learning, in: American Psychologist, 11/1954, 221-233

Spitzer M.(2006): Vorsicht Bildschirm, Berlin

Strittmatter P. - Niegemann H. (2000): Teaching and learning with media. An introduction, Darmstadt

Süss D. - Lampert Cl.- Wijnen Chr. (2010): Media Education. An introductory study book, Wiesbaden

Swoboda W.H. (1994): Media education. Conceptions, problem horizons and fields of activity, in: Hiegemann S. - Swoboda W.H. (eds.): Handbuch der Medienpädagogik. Theoretical Approaches - Traditions - Fields of Practice, Research Perspectives, Opladen, 11-14

Wagner W. (2014): Media literacy revisited. Media as tools for appropriating the world, Munich

Watson J.B. - Rayner R. (1920): Conditioned emotional reactions, in: Journal of Experimental Psychology 3/1920, 1-14

Wilbers K.- Hohenstein A. (Eds.) (2010): Handbuch E - Learning, 32nd Supplement, Deutscher Wirtschaftsdienst Cologne, 1-20

Wolling J. (2009): Individualization of media use. Perspektiven der Forschung, in: Schade H. - Walterscheid H. - Wolling J. (eds.): Individualisierte Nutzung der Medien, Tagungsband Medienforum, Ilmenau 2008, Ilmenau University of Technology, 20-21 June 2008, Ilmenau, 7-18

Part III Artificial Intelligence

Introduction

We read a lot about artificial intelligence/AI and expectations are high. With the presentation of "Chatbot Chat GPT" by the company Open AI/San Francisco in November 2022, AI was registered by the public and the possibilities were highlighted and put up for discussion.

IT note > https://www.trend.at/unternehmensprofile/openai (17.11.2023)

Hopes and fears are expressed in a similar way to the development of technical progress in human history.

- In the past, machines performed physically demanding work in industry, construction and agriculture, for example.
- Today, for example, AI performs translations, research and complex analyses. Without autonomous consciousness, AI is a powerful instrument that can significantly damage democratic discourse (cf. deep fakes, falsification of votes, perpetuation of prejudices). AI is the machine that learns from us and not the other way around.

Theoretical and practical considerations in the field of education are therefore necessary for political education (see Bundeszentrale für politische Bildung, Aus Politik und Zeitgeschichte 42/2023 "Künstliche Intelligenz").

The following considerations are based on

- the topicality,
- an examination of the specialist literature in the context of political education and
- exemplary participation in online training in the quaternary education sector.

With regard to technological and socio-cultural development, the study is intended as an approach to the complex topic in the context of political education.

IT notes

AI in schools - the future of teaching and materials

● https://www.betterteachingresources.com/post/kÃ¼internet-intelligence-teaching (21.11.2023)

Understanding basic digital education in adult education institutions●

https://link.springer.com/article/10.1007/s40955-023-00235-z

(21.11.2023) AI at universities

https://hochschulforumdigitalisierung.de/sites/default/files/dateien/HFD_AP_5 9_Kuenstliche_Intelligenz_Hochschulen_HIS-HE.pdf (21.11.2023)

AI rules in the EU

● https://orf.at/stories/3342229/ (9.12.2023)

1 Reflections on intelligence

The question is often asked whether AI can replace humans.

At the beginning of the 1980s, attempts were already being made to make computers intelligent. When it came to translations, it became clear that IT programs had difficulties translating based on rules. Maintenance resulted in major problems in correcting errors (cf. ZWEIG

2019; 2023, 04).

1.1 Machine learning Learning

Current AI systems work differently. They use past data and statistical methods to search for patterns that can be used in the future. These methods are referred to as "machine learning". The rules are not specified by humans, but rather used by machines according to statistical methods from data.

The machines are programmed by humans as to what is present in the available data and how often. The form in which the patterns or rules found are stored is also defined.

A simple example of this is the creation of a decision tree from data. Each question produces a large amount of data and measures the possibilities of homogeneous subgroups when asked about a certain characteristic. This process is not just about collecting data, you can also use input data.

1.2 Neural networks

This applies to "neural networks". It is a mathematical formula. A single number is calculated using a large amount of input data. Each neuron is weighted as a number, which is calculated as a new number. The changed weights of all neurons create a system. This allows layers to be built up with lots of data and quality. Objectivity does not exist in this way. AI systems can therefore not be reliable and comprehensible in their calculations, only then could they replace humans (cf. ZWEIG 2023, 06).

The new AI systems go through two phases.

- A training phase with data selected by humans from the past using a statistical method to automatically select rules forms a decision aid/"neural network" in a certain form/"statistical model". The "intelligence" lies in the order of the questions and the weighting of the formulas.

- The second phase uses these rules to calculate a decision, write a text, pixelate an image or produce audio data, for example.

Decision-making processes and communication about decisions are missing in AI systems. This results in the following problem: reliability and traceability.

Decision-making requires reliability in use, which is what rational people would do. Observing the machine in different situations is necessary for decision-making. This is essential in situations where the quality of the decision cannot be evaluated.

"Singular decisions" as phenomena without historical precedents are particularly interesting in civic education, such as those in the coronavirus pandemic, as there is a lack of practice data. AI systems can therefore not replace human decisions (cf. ZWEIG 2023, 07). Politics always involves value judgments, such as performance assessments in the field of education in their discrepancy in comprehensibility.

Reliability must be checked differently in the behavior of the machine. A probability in risk calculations, for example, is easier to create in selected cases. It is very easy to calculate "facts", i.e. statements with intersubjective findings.

There are also AI systems that generate something ("generative AI" > https://de.linkedin.com/learning/was-ist-generative-ki-22860708/unterschied- between-generative-ki-and-other-ki-forms [20.11.2023]). These include Chat GPT, which for example language programs/ texts, mid-journey/ images, audio files and translations from descriptions. The question of replacing creative activity remains open.

Creativity as a way of developing something new requires a machine with the latest trends and data. Such learning is based on association processes with all the weaknesses in an association. In any case, such a production would be difficult. People and human creativity cannot be replaced by AI systems in the coming years (cf. ZWEIG 2023, 08).

1.3 Intelligence in AI

Chat GPT raises questions about how intelligent AI is and what dangers it poses. Different answers are given. The term "intelligence" is difficult to grasp because intelligence is not an objective property of a system.

- IQ only applies to the rational or cognitive intelligence of people. Intelligence in general terms is the ability of a system to respond to input signals from the environment with output signals that increase the system's benefit from interaction with the environment (cf. OTTE 2023a, 09).

- General intelligence with inanimate systems/AI systems are machines. According to OTTE (2023a, 09), both terms are considered for the meaning of artificial intelligence/AI.

The framework of AI refers to physically generated systems that subsequently result in a classification of intelligence (cf. OTTE 2023a, 09-16).

Level 1 - deductive intelligence (mathematical, logical intelligence) Level

2 - inductive intelligence (learning intelligence)

Level 3 - cognitive intelligence (combined deductive and inductive intelligence)

Level 4 - conscious intelligence (perceptual intelligence)

Level 5 - self-aware intelligence (self-perceiving intelligence) Level 6 -

sentient intelligence (biological intelligence)

Level 7 - volitional intelligence (explicit volitional intelligence)

Level 8 - self-confident, willing intelligence (humanistic risk intelligence)

1.4 Summary

The risks of AI exist and are increasing (cf. OTTE 2023a, 16). Technical dangers are not actually to be expected, as singularity hardly ever occurs.

Of course there are dangers for people, think of surveillance through "social scoring" or "profiling", the fallibility of AI systems from level 2, the importance of human rights and human dignity.

The risk of increasing machine intelligence from level 3 onwards requires the dangers and scenarios to be recognized with clear social goals that should be defined as supranationally as possible:

The EU's draft "AI Act" only concerns level 1-3 AI software/systems > https://digital-strategy.ec.europa.eu/de/policies/european-approach-artificial-intelligence (21.11.2023).

AI is intelligent, artificial and physically produced. It simulates the intelligence of deduction, induction and cognition. The rational IQ is around 80. The intelligence of AI is low compared to the intelligence of living beings because there are other forms of intelligence in addition to cognitive intelligence.

In the natural analog environment, today's AI generally does not meet the requirements (cf. OTTE 2023a, 16).

2 AI and ethics

Exemplary questions such as the use of chat GPT in scientific work and robots raise ethical issues. The complexity of AI leads to certain contexts in ethical issues such as socio-technical, political and economic systems (cf. STAHL 2023, 17-22).

2.1 Concepts of AI

Defining AI is not easy. The term was introduced in 1956 by the mathematicians and computer scientists John Mac CARTHY, Marvin MINSKY, Nathaniel ROCHESTER and Claude SHANNON, who assumed that machines could simulate any aspect of learning or any other characteristic of intelligence (cf. MC CARTHY; MINSKY, ROCHESTER, SHANNON 1955/ 2006, 13; STAHL 2023, 17).

As properties of intelligence are Language, abstractions and concepts, problem solving and self-improvement.

According to STAHL (2023, 17-18), three uses of AI are proposed as an experiment

- machine learning
- converging/ interdisciplinary socio-technical systems and
- General AI or Artificial General intelligence (cf. >https://arxiv.org/abs/2303.12712 [22.11.2023] < https://topos.orf.at/hirn-und-amir-ki100 [28.11.2023])

2.2 Ethical Issues

Ethical questions serve to describe different phenomena in the form of intentions, general statements and reflections (cf. STAHL 2023, 18). In German-speaking countries, a distinction is made between morality (generally recognized values) and ethics (theoretical reflection).

In the ethics of AI, differentiation is not widespread internationally. The many theories include virtue ethics, duty-based approaches to action, feminist ethics and religiously based ethics. A good part of the discussions in AI revolve around the development of general principles. In the various approaches, these include transparency, beneficence, justice, fairness, non-compensation, responsibility, privacy, beneficence, freedom and autonomy, trust, sustainability, dignity and solidarity.

The EU Commission's 2018 expert group proposes a framework for trustworthy AI that consists of legally compliant, ethical and robust AI and is generally recognized (cf. STAHL 2023, 18-19).

IT notes

EU framework for AI > ● https://www.bundeskanzleramt.gv.at/themen/europa- aktuell/2023/06/ki-gesetz-parlament-beschliesst-rahmen-fuer-kuenstliche- intelligenz.html

[22.11.2023] > ● https://eur-lex.europa.eu/legal- content/DE/TXT/?uri=CELEX:52023DC0206 [29.11.2023] > ● https://orf.at/stories/3342229/ [9.12.2023]).

2.3 Opportunities and risks

A discussion of ethical aspects requires the two aspects of advantages/opportunities and problems/risks.

- Advantages/opportunities - economic impact, higher efficiency and productivity, prosperity - processing of large amounts of data

- Risks/ problems - disagreement in a pluralistic society about the realization of AI - opacity - unpredictability/ data protection

A key ethical question arises

- from the converging/interdisciplinary socio-technical systems with the characteristics of social impact and autonomy, including human behavior/manipulation, dependencies. They raise numerous social and political questions concerning the use of socio-technical systems (cf. use of technologies; STAHL 2023, 20). This makes civic education a pedagogical responsibility (cf. economic education).

- The sensitive problem areas of information and communication are also affected (cf. media use/media literacy, withdrawal vs. creation of spaces for democratic participation, medical care).

2.4 Eco-potential

AI has enormous economic potential. Increasing prosperity does not automatically lead to fair distribution.

The target groups addressed are consumers/individuals, private and public institutions/companies, state administration and civil society organizations of all kinds - regulatory measures, legislation (cf. STAHL 2023, 22).

An example of a national and international approach is the EU's "AI Act". The need to integrate economic, political and social systems as a question of the ethics of AI is intended to achieve socially desirable conditions.

This leads to specific analyses of ethics (see, for example, analytical ethics according to FRANKENA 1981 > ● http://www.netzwerkgegengewalt.org/wiki.cgi?Ethik#8AnalytischeEthik [23.11.2023]). There are no uniform (simple) answers to the areas addressed; rather, they must be answered in a context-specific manner.

The constellation in AI results from the sub-areas of technology, application and social context.

3 AI and democracy

AI development has a reputation for being highly disruptive. It improves existing processes and changes the view of developments and goals of socio-economic activity. If the internet, socio-cultural networks and the smartphone have brought about changes, the public discussion of chat GPT will reach a peak at the end of 2022.

In the following, technological development refers to democratic discourse (cf. THIEL 2023, 23-28).

3.1 New developments

AI is not a single technology; rather, it is a categorical term for a technological process that solves complex processes in line with the situation (cf. THIEL 2023, 23).

It is necessary to analyze how social communication and processes change when different actors interact (cf. HOFMANN 2022 > https://digid.jff.de/demokratie-und-ki/ [22.11.2023]; PASCHER - PACK - HOMOLKA 2024, 4).

From the middle of the 20th century, there were two different approaches to implementing AI (cf. THIEL 2023, 23-24).

- Approaches with classification/"symbolic AI" for processing data
- Connectionist approaches using machine learning and neural networks to analyze problems/ patterns and probabilities

Around 2010, the upswing in AI began again with access to large amounts of data, large computing capacity and improvements in image recognition and/or language models/translations. The questions of the opportunities for action promoted by the technology, such as socio-economic incentives, political regulations and social/sociocultural uses, remained open (cf. BERG - RAKOWSKI - THIEL 2022, 171-191).

3.2 Political participation

Previously, the discussion focused on the implementation of a democratic public sphere through AI processes/moderation of social network content. As a result, an awareness of the dynamics of change was created. Information and communication are subject to manipulative possibilities.

First, there is the fear of an increase in disinformation / misinformation with the challenge for a democratic discourse.

- In German-speaking countries, the democratic public sphere is characterized by a pluralistic media system, alternative communication options and a broad education system (cf. the area of responsibility of political education).
- Potential dangers lie in the overflowing information environment, erosion of the structural conditions of the democratic public sphere and changes in media use (cf. THIEL 2023, 25).

Without clear regulations to ensure control and accountability, AI procedures undermine democratic procedural guarantees (cf. THIEL 2023, 27).

Social use of AI processes is of interest for political participation (codetermination, co-responsibility).

Elements include the promotion of communication - bringing debates together, procedural support for politics - citizenship, expansion of political marketing (cf. the potential dangers of technocratic depoliticization).

The outlined development stages/possibilities of democratic practice in the assumed increasing importance of AI processes result in different representations.

An analysis reveals a picture of active political shaping with limitations. Concrete democratic dimensions are to be addressed, with the possibility of shaping, whereby a liberal imperative is to be assumed (cf. the EU example of Estonia). The socio-cultural, socio-economic and technological elements are challenged in the context of political education with its many reference areas.

4 AI and the world of work

The way of life and the world of work changed massively with the Industrial Revolution around 250 years ago, and human work was reorganized through the use of machines. In this context, we speak of a "machine age" (see INSTITUTE FOR THE HISTORY AND FUTURE OF WORK/ IGZA 2023 > https://igza.org/publikationen/ [24.11.2023]).

There is a discrepancy between the growing technical possibilities of digitalization and an understanding of its useful applications. The advantages and disadvantages are closely linked to politics and the economy. We are in the middle of the effects on work, time, income and quality of work. "It is of central importance how politics and business steer the development and distribute the benefits of AI and increase the quality of work" (KELLERMANN - MARKERT 2023, 35).

4.1 Development of automation

For the use of AI in the world of work, the development over the past 200 years with the economic framework conditions is of interest.

- Since 1800, the amount of goods produced in one hour has roughly tripled in Germany, the USA and the UK (cf. IGZA 2023, vol. 3, 55).

- The annual working time fell from over 3000 hours in the 19th century to 1588 hours today (see working time calculation 2023 > https://iab.de/daten/iab-arbeitszeitrechnung [24.11.2023]).

- There was a phase of expansion after the Second World War, but growth rates leveled off again from 1970 onwards. The technology of the early/first machine age was applicable in material production, automation in other sectors was still lacking. The full use of AI technology is yet to come. "General purpose technologies (GPTs)" need a start-up phase and require supplementary investments, complementary technology and reorganization of processes and operations (cf. KELLERMANN - MARKERT 2023, 35).

- Compared to the steam engine as an energy source, digitalization is developing rapidly. Around 4.7 billion people worldwide own a smartphone, with the iPhone having just been launched by Apple around 16 years ago (see > https://de.statista.com/themen/581 [25.11.2023]).

- The speed and performance gains of data processing machines have reached an extraordinary level of dynamism and technological development (see IGZA 2023, Vol.7, Data Manual, 131-132).

- The increase in productivity did not lead to unemployment; on the contrary, work shifted to other sectors, job profiles changed and new occupations were created (cf. KELLERMANN - MARKERT 2023, 36).

4.2 Supplementary functions of the AI

The complementary assistance functions of data-driven systems, such as human-robot collaboration, 3D printing and additive manufacturing, have become an important part of the discussion. Assistance systems are changing the activities, meaning and qualifications of a profession.

In addition to educational aspects of career choice in the context of educational guidance, this is where the importance of AI and work comes in. This is triggered by developments in generative language models such as Chat GPT on the labor market. Teaching professions, media professions and PR professions as well as professions in management and the entertainment industry will have the highest shares for partial automation through generative AI. The ILO estimates that a quarter of office jobs will be performed by language models with gender-specific effects (cf. KELLERMANN - MARKERT 2023, 38-39).

The high degree of substitution in certain areas of activity characterizes the media reports (see, for example, the innovative capacity of Chat GPT vs. brainpower, Salzburger Nachrichten/ SN 18.11. 2023, 15).

Press release SN 18.11.2023, 15 "Chat GPT vs. brainpower. Who is more innovative? Artificial or human intelligence?"

There are now virtually no limits to artificial intelligence. It creates sophisticated texts, analyzes financial data or answers customer queries automatically in the shortest possible time - and with astounding quality. Numerous "white - collar" professions are therefore currently under scrutiny and many people are afraid of losing their jobs.

But can AI also innovate? What about entrepreneurial achievements such as creating an innovation strategy? Nikolaus Franke, Academic Director of the MBA Entrepreneurship & Innovation Academy, recently put this to the test with 21 MBA students. They were given five minutes to draw up an individual proposal on how to react if a small company has an outstanding innovation idea but is unable to protect it. The time was so short that they basically had to start writing immediately - they only had a good second for each word. It was basically impossible to think and reflect. The reason for this extreme time restriction was that the students were to be given similar conditions to Chat GPT.

As expected, Chat GPT completed the tasks very quickly, but only managed to get close to the maximum 200 words allowed on the fifth attempt. The anonymized solutions, which did not reveal whether they came from students or Chat GPT, were evaluated by two scientists with several years of experience in the field of entrepreneurship and innovation. The result was clear: although the MBA students proposed very different strategies - sometimes they focused on consistent branding as an innovator, sometimes they suggested a step-by-step approach initially in market niches in order to attack the main market from there - sometimes they recommended cooperation with a retail company - their solutions were clearly superior to AI. The MBA strategies were given an average score of 2.4. Chat GPT's strategy was a somewhat diffuse mixture of all kinds of strategy elements and was therefore given an extremely moderate score of 4.5.

However, Nikolaus Franke is convinced that the poor performance should not be misinterpreted: "Generative AI such as Chat GPT is a fundamental innovation with disruptive potential and is therefore extremely important, especially for entrepreneurs. Countless subtasks in the entrepreneurial process can be completed better, faster and with fewer errors with the help of artificial intelligence." In the WU Executive Academy's MBA programs, its use is not fought against, but intelligently promoted.

The automation of the latest developments results in changes to job profiles because tasks are eliminated, new ones are added and/or weighted differently or new occupations are created. In the USA, around 80 percent of employment in 2018 was in occupations that did not even exist in the 1940s (see DAVID 2022; KELLERMANN - MARKERT 2023, 39).

Social policy issues arise in the case of low qualifications, which can contribute to a polarization of income and career opportunities.

In this context get increasingly importance vocational training measures such as

- Educational and study counseling with coaching,
- Further training and support measures with the
- Aim of the political education a democracy-oriented lifelong education.

5 Challenges for the education sector

Learners/students and teachers are confronted with innovative methods and new forms of the education system in their educational and professional careers.

5.1 Changes over the decades

Just think of the introduction and use of computers in the 1980s and the changes that have taken place in recent decades.

The much-vaunted digital revolution in the education sectors of schools and adult education, as well as in higher education with its equipment and support, took a long time. AI will hardly be able/need to come to terms with the length of this development phase.

Digital tools require considerable additional effort, such as dedicated premises, installation of programs and specialist knowledge with media skills (cf. NUXOLL 2023, 41-45).

5.2 Advantages of digital learning processes

AI is certainly worthwhile for

- Solutions for complex problems,
- Heterogeneity in learners/learning speed, abilities and needs,
- limited time resources, corrections and counseling sessions,
- sustainable learning/exercises, repetition and social learning,
- Performance assessments/project work, technical papers and seminar papers and
- alternative audit and assessment methods (see TRAUTWEIN - SLIWKA - DEHMEL 2018).

The use of AI in education requires a distinction to be made between generative artificial intelligence/ chat GPT and intelligent tutoring systems/ ITS.

- Generative AI are models like how to generate chat GPT with texts, answering simple questions and creating complex essays.
- Intelligent Tutoring Systems (ITS) offer personalized learning, simulating the experience of a one-to-one lesson with a tutor in a subject area. Learning progress and deficits are recognized and targeted exercises and explanations are offered. Learning paths can be created. It should be noted that there are only a few German-language tutoring systems (cf. NUXOLL 2023, 42).

Data encryption and clear access guidelines must be ensured in educational institutions.

5.3 Pedagogical challenges

The following five aspects of a didactically based pedagogical task are the basis for dealing with digital learning and teaching.

An educational institution without teachers will continue to be a poor educational institution in the future, as will an educational institution without AI (cf. KELLERMANN - MARKERT 2023, 46).

- Neutrality - neutral and fact-based programs
- Reliability vs. disinformation or misinformation - factually based information
- Inequalities - access to technology, internet connectionand training in its use
- Dependence - risk of restricting AI and promoting own activities for experiments and innovations
- Accompaniment and support - joint learning and social interaction

Basically, media competence is part of the task.

6 Documentation training

Frau/Herr

Günther Dichatschek

hat an folgendem Seminar teilgenommen:

Die/Der Lehrende als Coach

von 29. bis 30. April 2008

Trainerin: Mag. Hildegard Köhler

Mag. Gerda Mraczansky
Leiterin Personalentwicklung
der Universität Wien

Seminarleitung

Teilnahmebestätigung

Universität Wien – Referat für Personalentwicklung, Maria Theresien-Straße 3/15, 1090 Wien
Tel.: +43 (0)1 4277 DW 12331, Fax: DW 12339, Email: personalentwicklung@univie.ac.at, www.univie.ac.at/personalentwicklung

Frau/Herr

Günther Dichatschek

hat an folgendem Seminar teilgenommen:

Kreative Entwicklung hochschuldidaktischer Methoden

von 9. bis 11. Dezember 2009

Trainer: Mag. Oliver Schrader
Mag. Michael Stadlober

Mag. Gerda Mraczansky
Leiterin Personalentwicklung
der Universität Wien

Seminarleitung

Teilnahmebestätigung

Universität Wien – Personalentwicklung, Dr.-Karl-Lueger-Ring 1, A-1010 Wien
T: +43 (0)1 4277 DW 12331 | F: DW 12339 | E: personalentwicklung@univie.ac.at, http://personalentwicklung.univie.ac.at

UNIVERSITÄT
SALZBURG

Zertifikat HSD+

Herr
Dr. Günther DICHATSCHEK, MSc

hat den

internen Lehrgang für Hochschuldidaktik

HSD+ Erweiterungslehrgang (WS 2015/16)

an der Universität Salzburg im Ausmaß von 2 ECTS-Credits erfolgreich abgeschlossen.

Salzburg, am 25. Februar 2016

Univ.-Prof. Dr. Jörg Zumbach
Lehrgangsleitung

Univ.-Prof. Dr. Erich Müller
Vizerektor Lehre

Ao.Univ.-Prof. Dr. Rudolf Feik
Vizerektor QM & PE

Personalentwicklung

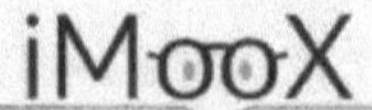

Teilnahmebestätigung

für

Dr. Günther Dichatschek MSc

Hiermit wird die Teilnahme an dem von CONEDU & PartnerInnen auf der Plattform iMooX angebotenen

EBmooc – Offener Onlinekurs zu digitalen Werkzeugen für ErwachsenenbildnerInnen

#ebmooc17

bestätigt.

Die Teilnehmerin/der Teilnehmer hat alle sechs Multiple-Choice-Tests erfolgreich bestanden.

Inhalt der Module

1. Einführung: Aufbau des EBmooc und das Lernen in MOOCs
2. IKT-Tools für die tägliche Arbeit rund um ein Bildungsangebot
3. Social Media in der Erwachsenenbildung
4. Blended Learning und eLearning in der Erwachsenenbildung
5. Offene Bildungsressourcen für die Erwachsenenbildung
6. Bildungsberatung (und Lernberatung) mit Online-Unterstützung

Der Zeitaufwand hierfür war mit 18 Stunden für das Selbstlernen veranschlagt.

VeranstalterInnen

Mag. [a] Dr. [in] Birgit Aschemann u. Mag. Wilfried Frei (Leitung), DI. [in] Martina Süssmayer | Verein CONEDU
Dipl.-Ing. Dr. Martin Ebner | Technische Universität Graz, Mag. David Röthler | Verein WerdeDigital.at

Graz/Austria, im April 2017

EBmooc erwachsenenbildung.at 2017 | #ebmooc17
von CONEDU, TU Graz und WerdeDigital.at | auf imoox.at
Gefördert aus Mitteln des Bundesministeriums für Bildung

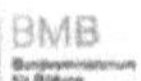

7 Bibliography AI

The titles that are used and/or directly quoted in the article are listed.

Berg S. - Rokowski N. - Thiel Th. (2022): The digital construction. A definition of position, in: Journal of Political Science 2/ 2022, 171-191

Federal Agency for Civic Education (2023): Journal Aus Politik und Zeitgeschichte - Artificial Intelligence, 73rd volume 42/ 2023, October 14, 2023, Bonn

David H. et.al. (2022): New Frontier: The Origins and Content of New Work, 1940-2018, National Bureau of Economic Research, NBER Working Paper 30389/ 2022

Frankena W.K. (1981): Analytical Ethics. An introduction, Munich

Kellermann Chr. - Markert C. (2023): AI in the world of work, in: Journal Aus Politik und Zeitgeschichte 42/ 2023, 35-40

Mc Carthy J.- Minsky M.- Rochester N.- Shannon Cl. (1955/ 2006): A Proposal for the Darmouth Summer Research Project on Artificial Intelligence, August 1955, in: AI Magazine 4/ 2006, 12-14

Nuxoll Fl. (2023): KI in der Schule, in: Journal Aus Politik und Zeitgeschichte 452/ 2023, 41-45

0tte R. (2021): Machine Awareness, Frankfurt/ M.

Otte R. (2023a): Intelligence and Consciousness, in: Journal Aus Politik und Zeitgeschichte 42/ 2023, 09-16

Otte R. (2023b): AI for Dummies, Weinheim

Pascher D. - Pack - Homolka St.(2024): Danger for democracy?, in: Salzburger Nachrichten, 20.1.2024, 4

Salzburger Nachrichten, November 18, 2023, CAREER, 15 : "Chat GPT vs. brainpower. Who is more innovative? Artificial or human intelligence? This question was recently posed to 21 students at the WU Executive Academy"

Schröder L. - Höfers P. (2022): Praxishandbuch Künstliche Intelligenz: Handlungsanleitungen, Praxistipps, Prüfragen, Checklisten, Frankfurt/ M.

Stahl B.C. (2023): Gray areas between zero and one, in: Journal Aus

Politik und Zeitgeschichte 42/ 2023, 17-22

Thiel Th. (2023): AI and democracy: Development paths, in: Journal of Politics and Contemporary History 42/ 2023, 23-28

Trautwein U.- Sliwka A.- Dehmel A. (2018): Basics for effective teaching, Stuttgart

Zweig K.A. (2019): It was the AI! From absurd to deadly: The pitfalls of artificial intelligence, Munich

Zweig K.A. (2023): Is AI threatening to replace humans?, in: Journal Aus Politik und Zeitgeschichte 42/ 2023, 04-08

Part IV Networking

1 Network against violence - Network for education

The website of the "Network against Violence - Network for Education" > http://www.netzwerkgegengewalt.org/wiki.cgi? < aims to establish a social network against violence.

The network was launched in October 2002 and has expanded thematically to include education since 2004.

- Networking complements efforts to meet educational challenges.
- Educational areas in their current importance and diversity determine the wiki project with a variety of topics.

Networking is important

- *from a European perspective* in the form of the
- "E - Platform for Adult Learning in Europe"/ EPALE > see https://ec.europa.eu/epale/de/resource- centre/content/network-against-violence
- cf. EPALE > https://epale.ec.europa.eu/de/node/152088
- *within the national framework* with
- of the "Continuing Education Academy Austria" > http://www.wba.or.at > Graduates > https://login.wba.or.at/absolvent_innen?user=13140
- In accordance with a teaching assignment, a network is established with the relevant institution that affects the department.
- Networking takes place in accordance with events at the Volkshochschule Tirol (cf. https://www.vhs-tirol.at/).

The web pages belong to a Wiki Web, i.e. anyone can comment on all pages and help write them, contribute new ideas and create pages.

Contributions and participants are welcome. This explicitly includes (but does not exclude) describing events and people, talking about studies and books, planning and reviewing projects or actions > http://www.netzwerkgegengewalt.org/wiki.cgi?Sammelbände

The original goal - to raise awareness of the connection between television and violence and to find ways to reduce exaggerated depictions of violence and glorification of violence - has become a sub-project within the larger context described above.

- Over time, education - initially in the context of violence - became a central issue.
- Scientificity and topicality are necessary.
- The focus is on personal interest.
- Criticism is welcome and must be justified.

Technical note: This website is a Wiki Web in which anyone can participate. Opposing opinions are also welcome if they are constructive. For more detailed instructions, see the user notes.

IT - Note

- http://www.netzwerkgegengewalt.org/wiki.cgi?

2 School Wiki

In the press, we often read about the need for pupils to acquire additional media skills. However, it is much rarer to read concrete examples of what this media literacy looks like and even less about how it should be taught.

An Internet connection for every school is nice, but it would be even nicer if it were put to good use. Let's take a look at how this can be done, clearly current reports from various newspapers or other news services, research on certain topics. But with these things, the providers are always different and the students are again only working for themselves, the grades and the teachers (if it were at least in that order). The results of the work are only accessible to the class and are only critically perceived by some of them, everything else is worthless.

However, there are projects on the Internet that anyone can work on and that are worth participating in. What's more, these projects can also be used to test interdisciplinary and cross-grade collaboration. The results are visible worldwide. And if the project reaches a certain size, they are not just the nice homepage of some school, but something permanent that will continue to be maintained, possibly even by the pupils when they have long since left the school.

Even better, the technical skills required for collaboration can be learned in much less than one lesson, even by students (or teachers) who don't want to have anything to do with computers.

The whole thing is called Wiki, which comes from the Hawaiian language and means fast. Just the way collaboration (technically) works there. A system in which anyone can change or write articles, in which links can be created quickly and a networked body of knowledge is created through the collaboration of many people. Of course, there is a great risk that a lot of nonsense will be posted there or that meaningful contributions will be spoiled, but experience has shown that the number of sensible participants far outweighs the number of bad ones, and every change is marked as such and can be undone.

Can teachers who are geared towards accuracy use this tool? This becomes a division of labor - creative people tackle the topics, planned people work them out, precise people remove the mistakes. Questionable content: If contributions are read, revised and corrected in detail by a community anyway, then the occasional reaction to an act of vandalism (1 - 2 per year and wiki) goes under as insignificant in everyday life.

But what potential is there: Pupils can ask questions. Parents can get involved. Classes from different schools could cooperate. Teachers from different schools could support each other in projects or with materials. Those affected could have their say in projects. It would probably not be difficult to produce a list of a thousand ideas, all related to the fact that a wiki is not a strictly administered system and that it is about new forms of engagement, participation and new social relationships. Some authors write about "social learning".

IT - Note

● http://www.schulwiki.org/wiki.cgi

To the author

APS teaching degree (VS - HS - PL 1970, 1975, 1976), certified school counselor (1975) and school development consultant (1999), member of the teacher examination commission for the APS at the Provincial School Board for Tyrol (1993-2002).

Graduate of Höhere Bundeslehranstalt für alpenländische Landwirtschaft Ursprung - Klessheim/ Reifeprüfung, Maturantenlehrgang der Lehrerbildungsanstalt Innsbruck/ Reifeprüfung - Studies in Educational Science/ University of Innsbruck/ Doctorate (1985), 1st Ecumenism course - Kardinal König Akademie/ Vienna/ Certification (2006); 10th University course in Political Education/ University of Salzburg - Klagenfurt/ MSc (2008), Continuing Education Academy Austria/ Vienna/ Diploma (2010), 6th University course in Intercultural Competence/ University of Salzburg/ Diploma (2012), 4th Internal course in Higher Education Didactics/ University of Salzburg/ Certification (2016). University course Intercultural Competence/ University of Salzburg/ Diploma (2012), 4th internal course University Didactics/ University of Salzburg/ Certification (2016) - Distance learning course Basic Course Adult Education/ Evangelische Arbeitsstelle Fernstudium, Comenius - Institut Münster/ Certification (2018), Distance learning course Sustainable Development/ Evangelische Arbeitsstelle Fernstudium, Comenius - Institut Münster/ Certification (2020).

Lecturer at the Institute for Educational Science/ University of Vienna/ Vocational Education - Pre-Vocational Education VO - SE (1990- 2011), Department of History/ University of Salzburg/ Teaching degree History - Social Studies - Political Education - SE Didactics of Political Education (2026- 2017).

Member of the Education Commission of the Evangelical Church of Austria (2000- 2011), Deputy Director of the Evangelical Education Center Tyrol (2004 - 2009, 2017 - 2019) - Course Director of the VHS Salzburg Zell/ See, Saalfelden and City of Salzburg/ "Freude an Bildung" - Political Education (2012 - 2019) and VHS Tyrol/ Basic Course Political Education (2024).

■m ailto:dichatschek@kitz.net

Printed by Books on Demand GmbH, Norderstedt / Germany